Guitar Picking Tunes
BLUES & JAZZ JAM TUNES

by William Bay

MW00565634

To Access the Online Audio Go To:

WWW.MELBAY.COM/WBM46MEB

Distributed by Mel Bay Publications, Inc.
WWW.MELBAY.COM

Contents

Preface

This is a collection of 48 original jazz tunes reflecting a variety of jazz styles. I wanted these melodies to be fun to play and also to lend themselves to jamming. I used a variety of keys and included tablature. There are few things more enjoyable than sitting down with other musicians and jamming. I hope you enjoy these pieces as much as I have writing and playing them.

William Bay

Idlin' on By

Jazz Waltz

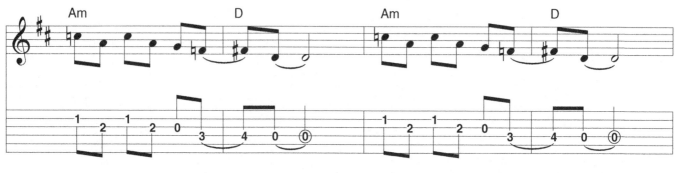

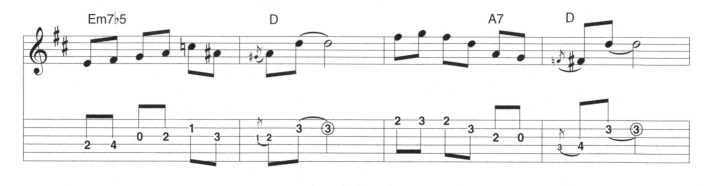

Jazz Breakdown

Cookin'

Be-bop feeling ♩ = *132*

W. Bay

Bop City

Breezin'

Blue Vibes

Riff for Clifford

Pacific Blues

Slow Groove ♩ = 120

W. Bay

Theme for Bird

Goin' Home Blues

Sauget Strut

Bistro

Funky George

15

Easy Blues

W. Bay

Minor Detail

Minor Groove

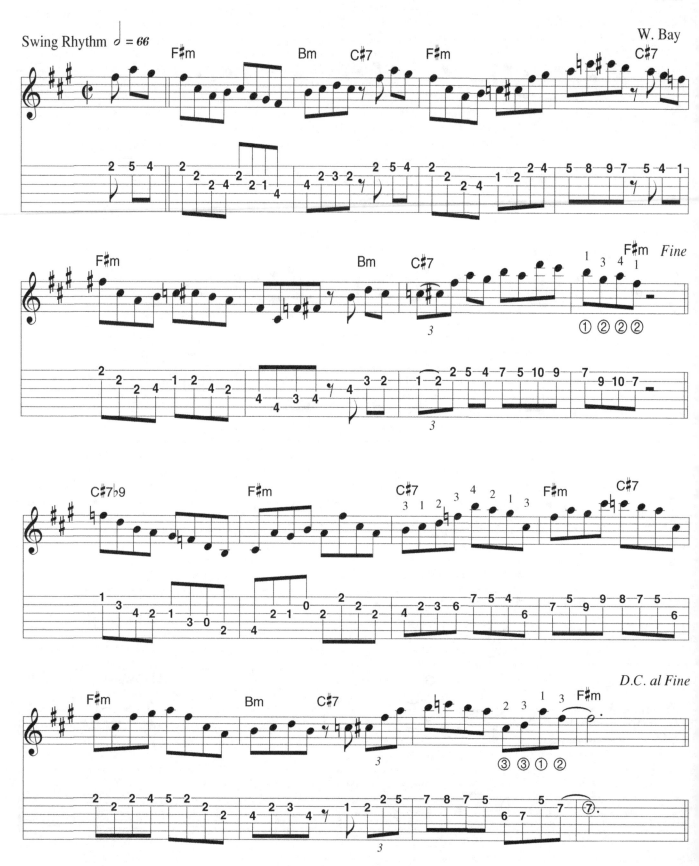

Cabin Fever

Groove Time

Cruisin'

Ee's Flat

W. Bay

Reel Jazz

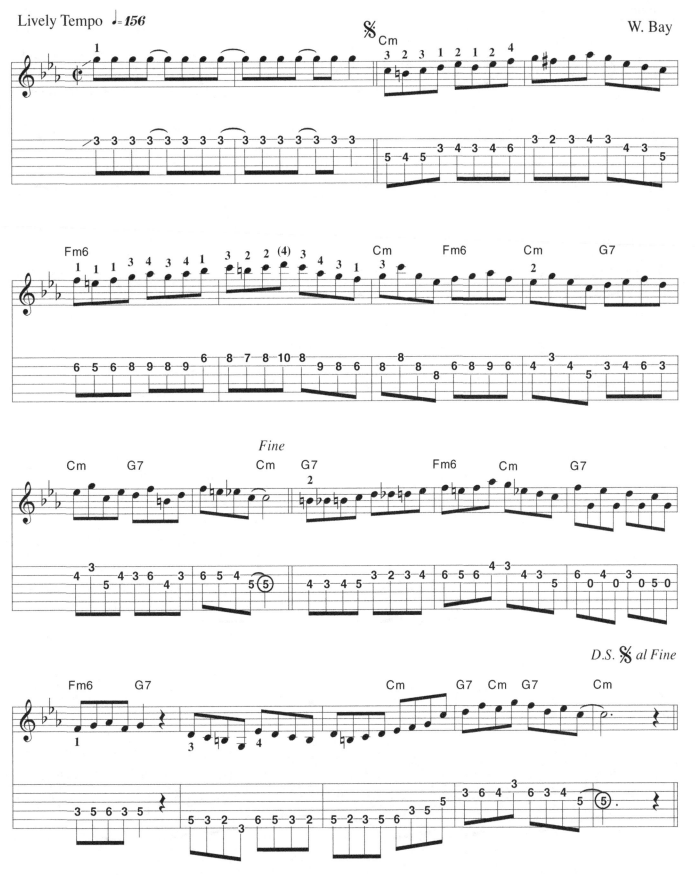

Jazz Etude

Slick Pickin'

Medium Jazz ♩=148

W. Bay

Vanguard

Revival Blues

For Wes

High Steppin'

Fast, Jazz Tempo ♩=*152*

W. Bay

Funky Mr. Green

Walkin'

Waltz for Wes

Hot Footin'

Hot Club

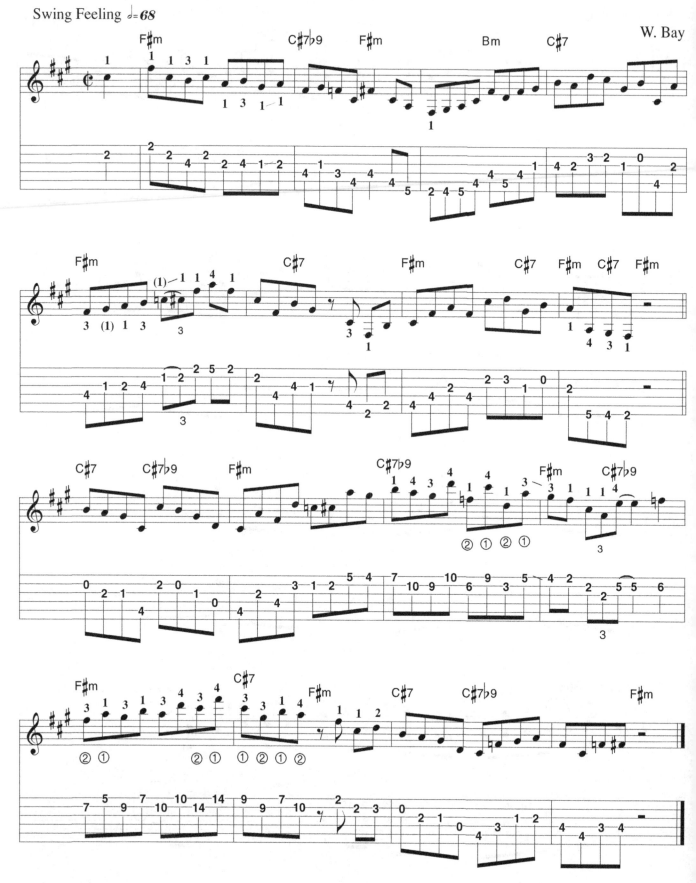

Waves

Double Time Feeling
Medium Jazz Rock ♩= 74

W. Bay

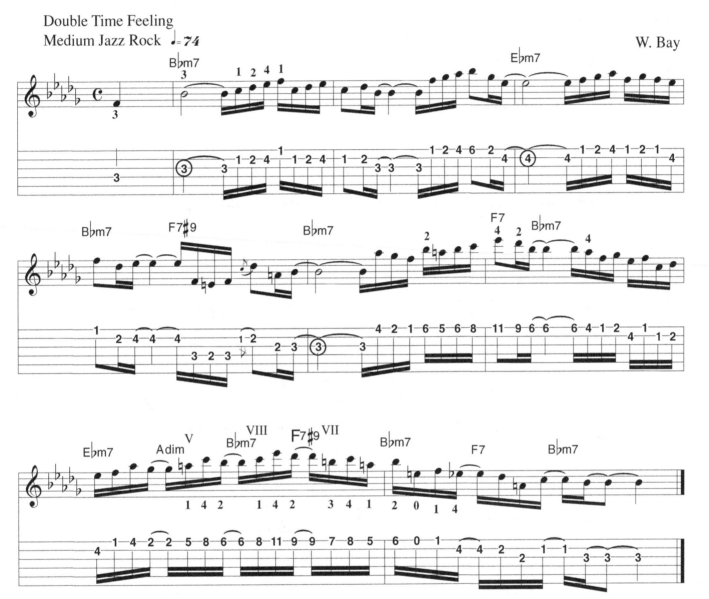

Easin' on By

Green Light

Swing Feeling ♩=160

W. Bay

Three Two = Five

Two Three = Five

Side Steppin'

Laguna Nights

42nd Street

40

Phantom Strut

On the Road

Shufflin'

Moderate Swing (♪♪ = ♪³♪) ♩=120

W. Bay

Later

Jumpin'

Cajun Spice

Swing Feeling ♩=142

W. Bay

46

Other Mel Bay Jazz Guitar Study Books

120 2-Bar ii-V Riffs (Vignola)
240 2-Bar Guitar Riffs (Vignola)
Achieving Guitar Artistry-Linear Guitar Etudes (W. Bay)
Achieving Guitar Artistry-Odd Time Etudes (W. Bay)
Achieving Guitar Artistry-Contemporary Baroque Etudes (W. Bay)
Achieving Guitar Artistry-Contemporary Picking Etudes (Pennanen)
Advanced Jazz Guitar Improvisation (B. Greene)
Complete Book of Jazz Guitar Lines & Phrases (Jacobs)
Complete Book of Jazz Single String Studies (Salvador)
Complete Guitar Improvisation Book (Bredice)
Essential Jazz Etudes/ The Blues for Guitar (Wilkins)
Essential Jazz Lines in the Style of Wes Montgomery (C. Christiansen)
Extreme Warm-Ups and Chops Builders for Guitar (Anthony)
Frank Vignola's Complete Jammin' The Blues Play-Along for Guitar
Frank Vignola's Complete Rhythm Changes Play-Along for Guitar
Fundamentals of Guitar (Miles Okazaki)
Getting Your Improvising into Shape (Becker)
Guitar Arpeggio Studies on Jazz Standards (Mimi Fox)
Graduated Soloing (Mimi Fox)
Guitar Journals: Jazz (Multiple Authors)
How to Play a Tune in Any Key (C. Bay)
Improvisational Techniques for Jazz Guitar (Umble)
Improvising with Mini-Arpeggios (Musso)
Jazz Intros and Endings (Eschete)
Jazz Guitar Essentials: Gig Savers Complete Edition (C. Christiansen)
Jazz Guitar Lines Workout (C. Christiansen)
Jazz Guitar Phrasing Workout (W. Bay)
Jazz Guitar Scale Chart (C. Christiansen)
Jazz Guitar Structures (Andrew Green)
Jazz Guitar Wall Chart (C. Christiansen)
Jazz Pentatonics (Saunders)
Jazz Scale Workout (Karsh)
Jazz Scales for Guitar (C. Christiansen)
Jazz Soloing Basics (C. Christiansen)
Jazz Structures for the New Millennium (Diorio)
Jazz Warm-Ups for Guitar (Anthony)
Learning Tunes Workout (Cummiskey)
Mel Bay Jazz Guitar Curriculum: Diminished Workbook (Saunders)
Mel Bay Jazz Guitar Curriculum: Payin' Your Dues with the Blues (Umble)
Mel Bay Jazz Guitar Curriculum: Moveable Shapes-Concepts for Reharmonizing ii-V-I's (Sheryl Bailey)
Melodic Improvising for Guitar (Saunders)
Melodic Minor Guitar ...USC Curriculum (Pat Kelley)
Modern Blues (Saunders)
Play-Along Jazz Standard Chords Progressions (Vignola)
Sight Reading for the Contemporary Guitarist (Bruner)
The Art of Picking (Jimmy Bruno)
The Changes (Sid Jacobs)
The Ultimate Map for Jazz Guitar (Anthony)

WWW.MELBAY.COM

Other Mel Bay Jazz Guitar Solo and Study Books

Barry Galbraith Guitar Solos Vol. 1
Ben Monder Compositions
Bucky Pizzarelli Master Jazz Guitar Solo Collection
Easy Jazz Guitar Solos (de Mause)
Howard Alden: Sweet and Lowdown
Improvising Solos for Guitar (Lawrence)
Jazz Blues Styles (Diorio)
Jazz Guitar Made Easy (C. Christiansen)
Jazz Guitar Standards (Multiple Authors)
Jazz Guitar Standards II: Complete Approach to Playing Tunes (Multiple Authors)
Jazz Solos Vol. 1 (Vignola)
Jazz Solos Vol. 2 (Vignola)
Kurt Rosenwinkel Compositions
Lionel Loueke: Original Compositions
Master Anthology of Jazz Guitar Solos Vol. 2 (Multiple Authors)
Master Anthology of Jazz Guitar Solos Vol. 3 (Multiple Authors)
Master Anthology of Jazz Guitar Solos Vol. 4 (Multiple Authors)
Soul Jazz Guitar (Randy Johnston)
Swing to Bop: The Music of Charlie Christian (Ayeroff)
The Jazz Guitar Stylings of Howard Roberts (M. Holder/Patty Roberts)
Vic Juris: Inside/Outside
Wes Montgomery: Best of Boss Guitar
Wes Montgomery: The Early Years
7-String Jazz Guitar Chord Chart (W. Bay)
21st Century Chords for Guitar (Bloom)
Basic Line Basics for Guitar (Chapman)
Coltrane Changes (C. Christiansen)
Comping the Blues (Vignola)
Complete Book of Harmony, Theory and Voicing (Willmott)
Complete Book of Harmonic Extensions for Guitar (Willmott)
Creative Comping Concepts for Jazz Guitar (Boling)
Deluxe Encyclopedia of Guitar Chords/Case Size (W. Bay)
Deluxe Encyclopedia of Guitar Chords/Full Size (W. Bay)
Deluxe Encyclopedia of Guitar Chord Progressions (Rector)
Drop 2 Concept for Guitar (Chapman)
George Van Eps Harmonic Mechanisms for Guitar Vol. 1
Guitar Journals: Chords (W. Bay)
In the Pocket: Playing in the Groove (C. Christiansen)
Jazz Band Rhythm Guitar (Forman)
Jazz Guitar Chord Chart (W. Bay)
Jazz Guitar Chords Made Easy (W. Bay)
Jazz Guitar Essentials: Gig Savers Complete Edition (C. Christiansen)
Jazz Guitar Photo Chords (C. Christiansen)
Jazz Guitar Chord Workout (C. Christiansen)
Jazz Guitar Comping (Andrew Green)
Joe Pass Guitar Chords
Modern Chords (Juris)
Modern Chord Technique (George M. Smith)

WWW.MELBAY.COM

Made in the USA
Las Vegas, NV
08 October 2023

78775303R00031